BLACK RHINOS

BY KRISTEN POPE

Published by The Child's World®
1980 Lookout Drive • Mankato, MN 56003-1705
800-599-READ • www.childsworld.com

Acknowledgments
The Child's World®: Mary Berendes, Publishing Director
Red Line Editorial: Editorial direction and production
The Design Lab: Design
Amnet: Production

Design Element: Shutterstock Images
Photographs ©: Kayt Jonsson/U.S. Fish and Wildlife Service,
cover, 1; Mark Rigby/iStockphoto, 4; Liam Burrough Wild/
iStockphoto, 6–7; iStockphoto, 8; Bildagentur Zoonar GmbH/
Shutterstock Images, 9; Shutterstock Images, 10; Kermit
Roosevelt/Library of Congress, 11; Josef Vostarek/AP Images,
13; Piotr Gatlik/Shutterstock Images, 14–15, 22; Stacey Ann
Alberts/Shutterstock Images, 16; Fuse/Thinkstock, 18–19;
Guillaume Bonn/Corbis, 20; Brynn Anderson/AP Images, 21

ISBN 9781631439643
LCCN 2014959635

Printed in the United States of America
Mankato, MN
July, 2015
PA02264

ABOUT THE AUTHOR

Kristen Pope is a writer and editor with years of experience working in national and state parks and museums. She has taught people of all ages about science and the environment, including coaxing reluctant insect lovers to pet Madagascar hissing cockroaches.

TABLE OF CONTENTS

CHAPTER ONE

AMAZING RHINOS

Black rhinos use mud to keep cool.

It is a very hot day. The black rhinos lie in the shade. Some **wallow** in a nearby watering hole. They roll in the mud. It coats their skin. The mud protects them from the sun and bugs.

Black rhinoceroses, or rhinos, live in Africa. Their **habitat** includes grasslands, **savannas**, deserts, and

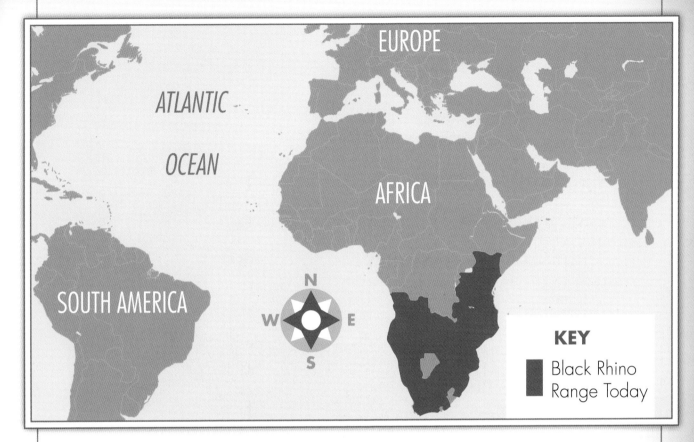

Black rhinos live south of the Sahara desert in Africa.

shrublands. Rhinos used to live across the southern Sahara, the world's largest desert. But now they are close to becoming **extinct**. Today rhinos can be found in 11 countries. But nearly all of them live in just four: South Africa, Namibia, Zimbabwe, and Kenya.

Black rhinos usually live within 15 miles (24 km) of water. They need to drink the water. But they also wallow in the mud and water to cool down. When there is water, rhinos drink every day. They also find places with salt and **minerals** to lick. This helps the rhinos stay healthy. Rhinos are **grazers** and eat only plants. They eat at night between dusk and dawn, when it is cooler.

Though they eat only plants, black rhinos are huge animals. They are up to 6 feet (2 m) tall at the shoulder. They can weigh more than 3,000 pounds (1,361 kg). Black rhinos hear and smell well.

Black rhinos eat plants, not meat.

Often, a rhino's first horn is longer than the second one.

Sometimes they find each other by sniffing along a trail. Most black rhinos have two horns. But some have three. The horn closest to the nose is usually the largest. Rhino horns can grow up to 3 inches (8 cm) a year. Some even grow to 5 feet (1.5 m) long. Males use their horns to fight off attackers. Females use their horns to protect their calves.

Female rhinos have their first calf when they are six to seven years of age. The mothers give birth every two and a half to five years. Mothers are pregnant for more than 12 months. Calves can be born any time of the year. They drink their mothers' milk for up to two years. Calves can live alone at approximately three years old.

BLACK AND WHITE RHINOS

Black rhinos and white rhinos both live in Africa. Black rhinos are gray, not black. They are closely related to white rhinos. White rhinos are gray like black rhinos, not white. Instead people can tell the two apart by their lips. Black rhinos have pointed upper lips. They use them to pull leaves from trees and bushes. White rhinos have square lips. They eat mostly grasses from the ground.

Adult black rhinos live up to 40 or 50 years. They usually live alone. But females may live in groups of up to 12. Males claim **territory** when they turn ten or 12 years old. Each male is the only one to live in his territory. Sometimes two males fight over a female. They may even battle to the death.

Black rhino calves live with their mothers for their first few years of life.

CHAPTER TWO

POACHING AND THREATS

People used to hunt black rhinos for fun.

In the early 1900s, there were hundreds of thousands of black rhinos. They roamed across parts of Africa. But over the years, humans killed many of these animals. Some rhinos were killed to make room for homes and farms. But hunters killed many

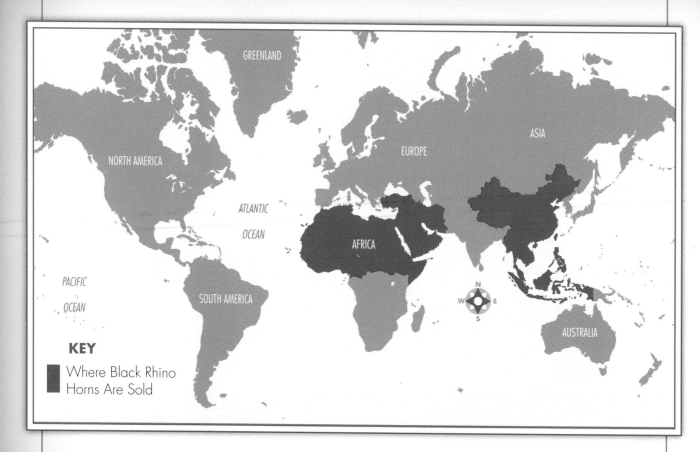

People in Asia, the Middle East, and Africa use rhino horns.

more for sport. By 1960 only around 100,000 black rhinos lived in the wild.

Between 1970 and 1992, **poachers** killed 98 percent of the black rhinos left in Africa. In just 22 years, more than 90,000 rhinos were killed. They are now **endangered**. In 2010 there were only 4,880 black rhinos left.

Poaching is the biggest threat black rhinos face. Poachers kill rhinos and take only their horns. They leave the bodies behind. Poachers sell the horns to make money. People in Asia, North Africa, and the Middle East buy them. Some use ground-up horns for a kind of medicine. This happens in Vietnam, China, Taiwan, Hong Kong, and Singapore. Others carve the horns as handles on special knives. This occurs in North Africa and the Middle East.

THE COST OF HORNS

Some people believe black rhino horns have special powers. They use the horns as medicine. These people are willing to pay a lot of money for rhino horns. In some Asian countries, rhino horns sell for tens of thousands of U.S. dollars. They can cost as much as gold.

Habitat loss is another threat. People continue to take over rhino habitat to build homes and farms. Others use the land for logging. They build roads in rhino habitat. Rhinos need access to this land for food and water. If people take over the places where rhinos find their food, rhinos cannot survive.

Humans have nearly caused the black rhino to become extinct. But some people are trying to save these large creatures.

With human help, black rhinos may once again roam African savannas.

CHAPTER THREE

SAVING BLACK RHINOS

Black rhinos need help if they are going to survive in the wild.

Humans have killed nearly all the black rhinos in the world. Today people are trying to save them.

In 1975 80 countries agreed to a law to protect many wildlife species. Now more than 180 countries have signed it. The law makes buying and selling rhino parts illegal. It is illegal to kill rhinos and take their horns. It is also against the law to bring their horns to other countries. But the law works only if people obey it. People do not always follow these laws. And police do not always **enforce** them.

Governments are working to better enforce these laws. Doing so will help stop the rhino horn business. Governments are learning more about the people who poach rhino horns. They are learning more about the people who buy and sell the horns, too. Many countries work together in this effort. That is because most poachers bring rhino horns to other countries to sell them.

People are hard at work keeping rhinos safe. They hope that doing so will increase the number of rhinos. People create **sanctuaries** to protect rhinos. These sanctuaries try to keep poachers away. Some even hire guards to do so. Being a rhino guard is a very dangerous job. Many poachers will kill people to get to the rhinos.

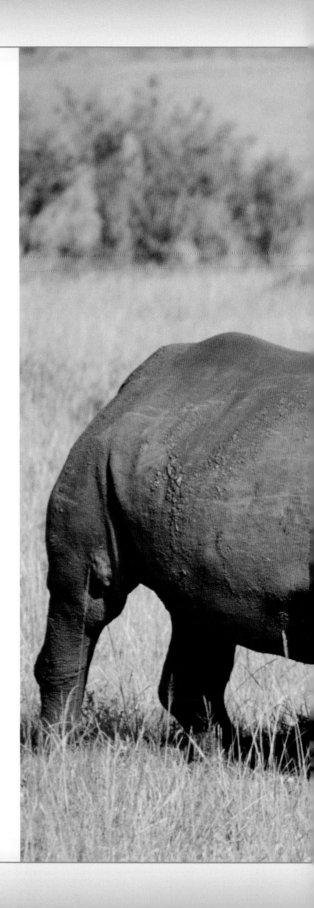

People must first get the rhinos to the sanctuaries. One way is to use **tranquilizers**. These drugs put the rhinos to sleep for a time. Once they are asleep, people can move the large animals. They use helicopters to get them to sanctuaries. This makes it hard for poachers to find the rhinos.

Technology helps rhinos, too. In Namibia scientists track rhinos with special radios. The scientists also have a special phone number. People call it to report poaching. They also call to name people who sell rhino horns.

Humans still have a lot of work to do to help save wild black rhinos.

RHINO SANCTUARY

The Black Rhino Range Expansion Project works to save rhinos. It started in 2003. Many groups and governments work together. The project houses rhinos on 37,000 acres (14,973 ha) of land. Since it began, the project has moved 120 rhinos there. Thirty new calves have been born there, too.

These people are preparing to move this black rhino to protect it from poachers.

Scientists in Kenya and South Africa study poached rhino horns. They try to discover who killed the rhinos. Police then use this information. They help put poachers and horn sellers in jail.

**Governments and people work to stop
the illegal sale of rhino horns.**

Many people in many countries work to help rhinos.
There are more wild rhinos now than there were a few
decades ago. But these animals are still in a lot of danger.
Since 2008 rhino poaching has increased more than
5,000 percent. There is still much work to be done to save
black rhinos.

WHAT YOU CAN DO

- Celebrate World Rhino Day on September 22.

- Never buy products made from rhino horn.

- Tell people what you know about black rhinos and that they are endangered.

- Hold a bake sale to raise money for rhino sanctuaries.

GLOSSARY

endangered (en-DANE-jerd) An endangered animal is in danger of becoming extinct. Black rhinos are endangered.

enforce (in-FORS) To enforce is to make sure people follow a law. Police and governments enforce laws protecting rhinos.

extinct (ek-STINKT) If a type of animal is extinct, all the animals have died out. The black rhino may become extinct if it is not protected from poachers.

grazers (GRAY-zurz) Grazers are animals that eat only plants. Black rhinos are grazers.

habitat (HAB-i-tat) A habitat is a place where an animal lives. People use black rhino habitat for homes and farms.

minerals (MIN-ur-ulz) Minerals are natural substances that are not animals or plants, such as salt, which animals need for good health. Black rhinos seek out salt and other minerals.

poachers (PO-churz) Poachers are people who illegally hunt and kill animals. Poachers kill rhinos for their horns.

sanctuaries (SANGK-choo-er-eez) Sanctuaries are natural areas where animals are kept safe from hunters. Some black rhinos live in sanctuaries away from poachers.

savannas (suh-VAN-uhz) Savannas are flat grasslands in warm regions. Black rhinos roam the African savannas.

territory (TER-eh-tor-ee) A territory is an area of land that an animal controls as its own. Male black rhinos claim territory after they are ten years old.

tranquilizers (TRAN-kwel-iz-urz) Tranquilizers are drugs that put an animal to sleep for a period of time. Scientists use tranquilizers to move black rhinos to sanctuaries.

wallow (WOL-oh) To wallow is to lie, roll around, or relax in water or mud. Black rhinos wallow to keep cool and stay away from bugs.

TO LEARN MORE

BOOKS

Borgeson, Grace. *Douwlina: A Rhino's Story*. Houston: Bright Sky, 2012.

Carson, Mary Kay. *Emi and the Rhino Scientist*. Boston: Houghton Mifflin, 2007.

Spelman, Lucy. *Animal Encyclopedia: 2,500 Animals with Photos, Maps, and More!* Washington, DC: National Geographic, 2012.

WEB SITES

Visit our Web site for links about black rhinos:
childsworld.com/links

Note to Parents, Teachers, and Librarians: We routinely verify our Web links to make sure they are safe and active sites. So encourage your readers to check them out!

INDEX